BLUFF YOUR WAY
IN
SEDUCTION

YVES CHÉBRAN

ℛℛ
RAVETTE PUBLISHING

Published by Ravette Publishing Limited
P.O. Box 296
Horsham
West Sussex RH13 8FH
Telephone: (01403) 711443
Fax: (01403) 711554

First printed 1989
Reprinted 1991, 1992, 1993, 1994, 1996

Series Editor – Anne Tauté

Cover design – Jim Wire
Printing & Binding – Cox & Wyman Ltd.
Production – Oval Projects Ltd.

The Bluffer's Guides® is a
Registered Trademark

The Bluffer's Guides® series is based
on an original idea by Peter Wolfe.

An **Oval Project**
for Ravette Publishing.

CONTENTS

The Art of Seduction 5
Seduction Combinations 6
Knowing the Motives 8
Adapting Your Style 17
Flirting 23
Foreign Seduction Techniques 24
Body Language 27

Seductive Types 29
Professional 29
Amateur (male) 30
Amateur (female) 32

Meeting 34
Opening Lines 35
Especially Seductive Places 37
Difficult Situations 38

She Seduces Him 42
The Setting 43
The Occasion 43
The Preparations 44
The Arrival 44
The Seduction 45
The Denouement 48

He Seduces Her 49
The Setting 49
The Occasion 49
The Preparations 50

The Arrival   51
The Move   53
The Finale   53

Useful Words and Phrases   55

THE ART OF SEDUCTION

To seduce is to tempt, entice or beguile someone to do something wrong, something foolish or something unintended. Leaving aside the something wrong and something foolish (for no bluffer would ever be party to anything illegal, immoral or possibly fattening), that really leaves unintended. But this is not quite accurate. The truth is that most seductions, at least those with any style (and the bluffer would naturally eschew all others), reach a point where both parties know exactly what is going on and what is likely to happen, even if it is only seconds before it does.

The two obvious players in any seduction are the Seductor and the Seductee. The word 'seducer' should be avoided since it is only ever used in a mildly insulting context, referring to someone who tries awfully hard but without much success. It also has strong connotations of villains with oil-slicked hair and black, waxed moustaches. And since many a Seductor is in fact female, the presence of a black, waxed moustache on her upper lip might well cramp her style.

Seductors and Seductees can also be divided into the Professional and the Amateur, whereas the seducer is merely incorrigible.

Professional Seductors may be male or female and exhibit a certain style, even panache. **Amateur Seductors** may also be either sex, but are allowed to show a certain natural charm, bordering on the gauche.

Professionals are never surprised when the seduction succeeds. Amateurs always are. Professionals are surprised when the seduction doesn't succeed; Amateurs console themselves with the fact that they and the other person involved can still be friends.

5

Amateur Seductors are those who haven't the ability, the style or the money to be a Professional Seductor.

The female **Professional Seductee** tends to be deeply romantic. The male equivalent is one who has built something of a social career on being a Seductee par excellence. He combines reasonable good looks with a shy, retiring nature and is often to be found working in the Arts where a touching vulnerability is combined with a deep sensitivity.

Amateur Seductees tend to be people who remember anniversaries, and keep diaries full of slowly disintegrating dried flowers. Whether male or female, they are essentially those who are too:

– naive
– tired, or
– uncomprehending

to realise what is going on. Even at the last they may simply regard the episode as 'something wonderful that just sort of happened.' Bluffers should always be kind to Amateur Seductees. Such innocence is rare these days.

Seduction Combinations

It is important to understand that the gap between the Professional (which is what you are on the way to becoming) and the Amateur, is as great as, possibly greater than, in any other occupation. NB: Always call it an art or an occupation. Never, ever, refer to seduction as a sport or a pastime or a hobby. Words like those put it on a par with spectator events, or collecting quite useless objects. Seduction is part of life itself, some would say the greater part, especially those with a natural bent.

There are four basic seduction combinations:

1. Professional Seductor/Professional Seductee

In this combination, both parties know what is going on. Both should have a good idea of the probable outcome within minutes of meeting. However, custom dictates that one or the other, and preferably the Seductee, should at least try to give the semblance of being amateur. It is not good form to be noticed mentally marking up the Seductor on style, presentation or degree of difficulty of his/her chosen technique. Indeed it could be said that a Professional Seductee is judged by how charmingly amateur he or she appears to be.

For example, a seduction begun while two people are jammed together in a crowded rush hour train: difficult. Specially if it takes place amidst the overpowering odour of the underground. While a seduction that begins with two fragrant people looking their very best, in a romantic restaurant, is regarded as being comparatively easy.

2. Professional Seductor/Amateur Seductee

This is the combination most favoured by Mills & Boon and by any Amateur Seductee with a grain of common sense, since they can be reasonably sure of Having A Good Time. As opposed to a Short Time . . . or Any Time At All.

Bluffers should note, however, that Amateur Seductees are allowed to recognise what is going on quite early in the proceedings without losing their amateur status. Nonetheless, this recognition should be accompanied by the belief that Something Wonderful/Unexpected/Deeply Meaningful Is Happening To Us.

3. Amateur Seductor/Professional Seductee

The proceedings here are characterised by the fact that the Seductee:

a) has nothing better to do that night
b) is feeling depressed and needs cheering up
c) has a strange sense of humour
d) may even genuinely be smitten.

4. Amateur Seductor/Amateur Seductee

This is the least thrilling scenario since it tends to lead to a certain amount of confusion when both simultaneously try to blow into each other's ears.

Yet bluffers should know that it is from combinations like this that a Professional Seductor often evolves. For the male this generally happens in that short space of time between being told by the Amateur (female) Seductee that she's really in love with someone else ... and being given the restaurant bill, which is always twice the amount expected; while Professional (female) Seductees evolve in the split second taken to realise that the Amateur (male) Seductor is actually proud to be wearing Y-fronts in the colours of Millwall Football Club. Thus the Amateur/Amateur combination usually results in at least one person determined to do better next time.

Knowing the Motives

Every bluffer must understand why people want to seduce, or to be seduced. With this knowledge you will be able either to:

● succeed, with consummate ease

● gracefully make your excuses and leave, if as sometimes happens, you realise that the whole idea is a Dreadful Mistake.

Seductors' Motives to Seduce

Seductors, of either sex, and whether Professional or Amateur, are primarily motivated by one or several of the following:

- Lust
- Ego
- Force of Habit
- Fame and fortune
- Mistaken identity
- The Television's Broken Down.

Lust

Lust is, of course, considered to be the primary motivation for a Seducer. However, even for those who can Think Of Little Else, seduction may be a cumbersome, time-consuming and expensive way of achieving their goal. This goes a long way to explain why Seductors of this sort plan for a denouement every bit as elaborate as the preliminaries themselves. Such elaboration is often wasted on the female Seductee however who, after much wining, dining and innuendo, would rather the Seductor just got on with it – and saved the chandelier swinging for another time.

Of course, female Seductors are also motivated by lust, but are not inclined to admit it. Their capacity for self-delusion is expressed as "I found him so devastatingly attractive, and so sensitive/humorous/intelligent/kind/sad/lonely too."

Ego

Ego, in association with all other motivations, plays a major role in the life of the Seductor. Often *the* major role, since for many Seductors the end is less important than the fact that they can still attain it.

Bluffers must bear in mind that many experienced Seductors argue forcibly that few, if any, seductions need actually end in bed. Simply having induced a desire to go to bed on the part of the Seductee, is prize enough. Besides, many an otherwise perfect seduction has come to a sticky end when words demand to be translated to deeds . . . and champagne corks aren't the only things that tend to pop off prematurely.

Many a Seductee has been left with nothing but the memory of a wonderful evening/few weeks that led absolutely nowhere. One or two have even been left with the bill.

Force of Habit

Habit motivates a number of Seductors who switch to automatic whenever someone vaguely attractive smiles at them. Sadly, such an individual often discovers too late that the Seductee does not live up to the promise; or is someone very special indeed who will expect the finest techniques that experience can give, and money can buy.

Force of Habit, if allowed to develop, can also ultimately become an unconscious action, namely Absent Mindedness. Here, the Seductor is not actually aware that he or she is apparently trying to seduce someone. No-one is more genuinely surprised than the Seductor (and occasionally a little alarmed) when confronted with an eager Seductee.

Word spreads and they can rapidly become the objects of derision. Worse, they can soon exceed the limit on their credit cards, without very much to show for it. Force of Habit is the type of behaviour that gets seduction a bad name. Bluffers should avoid it at all costs.

Fame and Fortune

The desire for fame and fortune is one of the oldest, some

would say one of the most honourable, seductor motivations. Detractors have labelled it simply 'sleeping one's way to the top', but bluffers should claim this to be the view of those who are:

a) Seductors who have failed, or
b) Seductees who have never been the object of any Seductor's attentions.

It is important to differentiate between the desire for fame and fortune as a Seductor per se, and using seduction to achieve those particular ends. The latter is perfectly acceptable, the former in exceeding bad taste; for the hallmark of the true Seductor – the Professional or the gifted Amateur – is that they never kiss and tell.

In addition, a reputation for being such a seductive individual places an almost unbearable burden on a Seductor. He or she could find themselves besieged by desperate Seductees, all determined to discover for themselves what the fuss is all about. This might sound alluring now, but it can lead to exhaustion, absent mindedness, and in the worst cases, premature retirement to a life devoted to studying the mating habits of the Californian fruit fly.

Bluffers should also realise that a seduction designed to achieve a material end does wonders for sharpening up one's technique. It is, in fact, a matter of applying the discipline of the market place; a healthy combination of business and art. Aside from all other considerations, seduction for fame and fortune rarely, if ever, results in a disappointed Seductee.

So, don't be selfish, remember your public, or at least, one of them at one special time.

The Television's Broken Down
Fate taking a hand is, in one form or another, probably the

11

most common Seductor motivation. To understand it, imagine you are at home with a friend watching television when it suddenly ceases to function. Feelings of annoyance, resignation and frustration pour over both of you. A stimulus has been snatched away. And, since nature abhors a vacuum, another one must be created to take its place.

Bluffers should note that the Seductee in this instance is rarely, if ever, someone who realises that he or she is a potential lover. In fact, research shows that in eight cases out of ten, the Seductee is usually the lover of one of the Seductor's closest friends, and the reason the two are alone together is:

a) so that they can discuss the strengths/weaknesses/failings of the absent lover
b) so that they can discuss certain problems that have arisen at work, or on a mutual project
c) the lover is away on business, or in hospital, and the Seductor is – at great cost to his/her personal life – Being Nice to the Seductee.

Remember, too, that if the seduction does take place, both parties can enjoy the moral consolation: "We were only thinking of someone else . . . but then things just got out of hand."

This, of course, is a near-perfect response since it tends to prevent guilt. Indeed, any guilt felt by the Seductee will probably be changed into resentment that the true lover was absent in the first place. In seduction, as in life, only the truly innocent are ever held to be fully culpable. Every Seductor, for example, is merely the victim of his or her own desires. Every Seductee is only the victim of circumstances.

Although seductions of this kind are largely unrehearsed, unscripted and somewhat of a surprise, the bluffing Seductor should always be ready for them, and to this end a certain amount of ethical 'planning' is permissible on the basis of: 'If it happens, fine, and if it doesn't, so what?' For example, in this instance, it would be a little silly for the Seductor and Seductee to be watching *Come Dancing*. The ideal programme would be something like *L.A. Law*, which combines strong elements of natural humour, drama, sex and romance in a thoroughly professional package – just like the best seductions.

Chance can occur in all sorts of circumstances. You don't actually need a dead television set, only a situation that appears to have nothing to do with a seduction – though the possibility should always be present. Working Late At The Office presents unlimited opportunity ("Oh, the copier's broken down"), but bluffers should check out the risk. Such a situation is fraught with tension if:

– the office is overlooked by a building site operating 24 hours a day
– the security staff are given to roaming freely through the offices at night
– the cleaners haven't started work yet.

Mistaken Identity
Mistaken Identity is a deeply shameful experience. Essentially, you, the Seductor, have either confused yourself with Casanova or Madame de Pompadour, or you have mistaken the Seductee for someone who really wants to be seduced. In reality the Seductee only wants to talk about the Corporation's next Five Year Plan. Or the political sub-text running through the works of Enid Blyton. Or a sick cat.

Alternatively, the Seductee may well be expecting a sublime experience which, with horror, you realise that you have no chance of providing. The subject is really too painful to discuss. It has sounded the professional death knell of many an established Seductor, and led them into permanent relationships, even marriage.

Seductee Motives to be Seduced

Seductees can have similar motivations to Seductors, albeit of a slightly less obvious kind, i.e.

lust – they love being desired
ego – they enjoy being flattered
force of habit – they're hopelessly absent minded
mistaken identity – they get carried away
chance – they adore surprises
fame and fortune – their dreams are all fantasy.

But bluffers should know that it is more likely that they are motivated by:
 – guilt
 – humour
 – compassion
 – boredom
 – curiosity
 – revenge
 – love.

Guilt
A professional Seductor can produce a host of guilt feelings in the Seductee, for example:

a)   guilt about not saying yes
b)   guilt for not realising what was going on
c)   guilt for having been considered in the first place.

And then there is the biggest guilt factor of all: the fact

14

that someone has gone to all that trouble, which they surely wouldn't have done unless they were pretty sure of getting a result. So all one can do is the decent thing and accept the role.

Sense of Humour
Often verging on the morbid, this is not to be confused with a sense of the ridiculous. Any Seductee motivated by humour basically finds everything highly amusing – and in so doing, manages to remain relatively untouched (in a spiritual sense of course) by the proceedings.

Compassion
This is an emotion usually borne by amateur Seductees, who will bare their heart, their soul and their body because of a deep sense of empathy with an unhappy, even tortured, Seductor (who in reality is anything but).

Bluffers should note that compassion plays little or no part in the amateur Seductee's frequent excuse "Well, I felt sorry for him/her." The truth is that the only thing the compassionate Seductee feels sorry about is that the seduction wasn't more fun.

Boredom
Boredom is often thought to be a main Seductee motive. Indeed, many Seductees appear to be bored at all stages, and only come to life to call themselves or their Seductors a taxi. However, bluffers know that in fact boredom is an offshoot of simple ego-gratification gone wrong. After all, being bored in bed is one thing, being bored *into* bed totally another. It is true, though, that professional Seductees are skilled at feigning boredom at most, if not all, stages of seduction since this encourages the Seductor to:

a) order champagne
b) offer them a job
c) happily accept the Seductee's excuse of a headache thinking that somehow it's probably their own lack of finesse that is making such heavy weather of the seduction. And usually, it is.

Curiosity
Is the Seductor as good as he or she is supposed to be? What is a professional seduction really like? These thoughts run through the curious Seductee's mind. And little else, for any Seductee motivated primarily by curiosity probably possesses the IQ of a lug-worm on a bad day.

Revenge
This usually takes the form of revenge on a lover or ex-lover who's been caught playing around. Seductees motivated by this type of revenge are liable to get the Seductor's name wrong, especially at moments of passion. Amateur Seductors will pretend not to notice; Professional Seductors will make it plain that they have, without saying so, and thus acquire the ammunition to induce many and useful guilt feelings on the part of the Seductee.

Love
Bluffers may be surprised at this one, but it does happen. A good many Seductees will be seduced for love, believing that the Seductor does return their affections, or will do so in future. Naturally, this is the last thing on the Seductor's mind, and may even inhibit the proceedings. Seductors are only human, after all, and dislike the inconvenience of being made to feel responsible for anyone else.

Adapting Your Style

Bluffers should be aware that long-term success in seduction results from convincing another that he or she:

- is going to have a good time
- is having a good time, or
- has had a good time

no matter what the reality of the situation.

Now that you are aware of the possibilities and the complexities of seduction, you can begin to put this knowledge into effect.

It is vital to vary your technique to fit the potential Seductee you are facing, or to know how to get out smoothly if you discover that he or she actually has the personality and/or chemistry of a skunk.

Remember, however, that whatever ruse you use, it should:

1. Exonerate you from all blame.
2. Leave the Seductee wanting to be seduced by you another time.

The Seductee is motivated by Lust

You are:

- warm
- sympathetic
- understanding
- and, initially, apparently oblivious to the Seductee's sexual charms.

As the seduction progresses, the Seductee becomes nervous, dispirited, and eventually slightly ashamed of his or her prurient desires. You then apparently, and suddenly, become aware of their sex appeal for the first time. You are drawn to them despite yourself. This places the Seductee in the apparent role of the Seductor. So if it all goes wrong, they have no-one to blame but themselves. (And they will. Every time.)

In nine cases out of ten, the sudden awakening on your part will have such an effect on the Seductee's morale as almost to result in abduction: yours.

How to Get Out of It
You can use a variety of ploys, ranging from:
a) getting the Seductee blotto
b) producing photos of children (they might even be your own) and if that doesn't do the trick, looking at them sadly as if conscience-stricken
c) claiming that you never kiss on a first date
d) developing a dreadful headache.

The Seductee is motivated by Ego
You are:
– flattering about their worst attributes
– dismissive of their best (but never unkindly)
– altogether charming
– (possibly) harbouring unrequited love for someone else.

The Seductee cannot help but be somewhat demoralised, but as ego is a stronger force than any other in no time at all he or she will see the seduction as a challenge, thus making you, the Seductor, the supreme prize.

How to Get Out of It
Talk about nothing but yourself.

The Seductee is motivated by Force of Habit
Bluffers should know that whatever they do, such a Seductee will act as if a seduction was taking place. Even if it's not.

How to Get Out of It
 - itemise the symptoms of a virulent social disease
 - offer to take him/her train spotting.

The Seductee is motivated by Absent Mindedness
Given that the Seductee is simply going through the motions, you should:
 - quickly learn to answer to another name
 - try and operate in total darkness.

How to Get Out of It
 - insist on being called by your own name
 - suffer sudden amnesia.

The Seductee is motivated by Fame and Fortune
This is all too simple, really:
 - hint at, but never admit to, being someone wildly influential
 - say how wonderful the two of you will be together
 - say how wonderful the two of you *are* together.

How to Get Out of It
State how wonderful it *has been* to be together – it doesn't matter when . . . within ten minutes of meeting will do.

The Seductee is motivated by the Television Breaking Down
You have, at the most, thirty seconds to make your move.

How to Get Out of It
You can't. In fact, you shouldn't even try until the seduction has reached its natural conclusion. Even then, it's considered polite to get dressed first.

The Seductee is motivated by Mistaken Identity
In other words, the Seductee thinks he or she is a great
lover. Or that you're a great lover. Either way, is looking
forward to a truly memorable experience. You can:
— develop a French accent
— disclose an interesting past.

How to Get Out of It
— Recite some unbearably crude limerick, and laugh
    loudly
— Develop a squint, tic or stammer.

The Seductee is motivated by Guilt
Remind yourself that Seductees of this sort are perpetual-
ly guilty. They enjoy being guilty. Life would be empty
without that comforting, dread feeling in the pit of their
stomachs. It would therefore be unkind of you to deny
them their pleasures. Whatever their reaction to your
advances, show disappointment. Make them feel guilty –
and they'll love it.

How to Get Out of It
— Refuse to accept the Seductee's guilt
— Claim that only the spoilt/immature feel guilty.

The Seductee is motivated by a Sense of Humour
Provided it's not you that's the sole object of the Seductee's
mirth:
— treat everything very light heartedly, but allow
    yourself to talk meaningfully, for a few minutes,
    about 'the comedy of life'
— never show any real emotion.

How to Get Out of It
- propose marriage, drawn up by contract
- invest (beforehand) in a squirt flower, or some other pointless practical joke, to aim at the Seductee
- begin to laugh at, as opposed to *with*, the Seductee. People like this often have no sense of humour about themselves.

The Seductee is motivated by Compassion
Sigh a great deal. Hint at some terrible tragedy in your life. Develop a limp. Let the Seductee know that he or she is the only person capable of bringing a moment's happiness into your life. Don't be ashamed to beg.

How to Get Out of It
- express contempt for the destitute/unemployed/Bob Geldof
- become so overwhelmed by the Seductee's concern for you that you simply must be alone for a while. But promise to telephone later. You never do.

The Seductee is motivated by Boredom
Nonchalance is the key. Your attitude must be that since life itself is pretty pointless, there's no real reason to do anything, or not to do something. Drift into the seduction, and preferably choose a rainy day.

How to Get Out of It
Fall asleep.

The Seductee is motivated by Curiosity
Suggest 'irresistible pleasure unendurably prolonged'. Never actually explain what it means. Ask the Seductee what he or she expects. Smile knowingly.

How to Get Out of It
Make use of such phrases as:
- "Oh, you're so sweet . . . so naive . . . so innocent."
- "This is wrong, you need someone of your own age" (particularly devastating if the Seductee is older than you).

The Seductee is motivated by Revenge
Never, ever, get caught up in a discussion about the Seductee's past lover. Be brutal in changing the subject each time it crops up. Remember, Seductees can talk all they like about their unhappiness with their friends. From you all they want is the knowledge that they're sophisticated, mature and sexy.

How to Get Out of It
- Claim that you have never felt/are incapable of feeling jealousy
- Suddenly remember that the ex-lover was a school friend
- (the umpteenth time the ex-lover is mentioned) say "I'm sorry, but three is a crowd" – and exit.

The Seductee is motivated by Love
Intimate that all things are possible: "Let's just see how it develops . . . I must admit I'm attracted to you . . . and you're someone I could love. But I've been hurt so badly . . . now I just need someone to be with."

If the Seductees swallow this, they really are in love. And if they are, it's not so much a seduction, more the lay of their life.

How to Get Out of It
Well, do you really want to?

Flirting

Flirting is an art which all would-be successful Seductors should perfect as an essential component of their art.

Handled by a professional, flirting indicates by the subtle employment of gesture and glance the following points:

- I find you exceedingly attractive
- If things were different, I'm sure we could make the most wonderful love together
- But since I'm/you're not free
- Please accept my admiration instead.

Whereas the amateur might signal in the most blatant way possible: "Cor! Fancy a bit?" The difference is obvious.

Many a flirt has developed into a full-blown seduction because the bluffing professional has, at the right moment, turned flirting from a compliment into a proposition by indicating: "Well, we've established that we find each other unbelievably attractive. So let's see each other again," or, "Any chance of losing your husband/wife/lover for an hour or so?" Note, however, that these questions are never actually said. They are hinted at, and much use is made of the eyes and innuendo.

The way in which bodies communicate, too, is vital, especially if the flirtee wishes to show that he or she is more than a little interested. Placing a hand on the other's arm, briefly, is a classic. As is standing face-on to a person. Or even brushing a hair off their clothes – or for a woman to straighten a man's tie. But nothing too obvious to outsiders. The essence of flirting is to create a closed, private world between the two of you.

Foreign Seduction Techniques

Bluffers should be aware of these – if only to be able to remark, knowingly:
- "See that couple over there? Any moment now and she'll pour her soup all over his amour propre."
- "Say what you like, but rough diamonds are a girl's best friend."
- "Ah the Latins! So romantic. So passionate. And so perverse."

French Seductors are given to being terribly civilised. Their problem is they cannot comprehend anyone, especially foreigners, not immediately being bowled over by their charm.

French Seductees. There are none. It is forbidden by the French constitution.

Italian Seductors roll their eyes a lot. At some stage the male Seductor will blame the female Seductee for leading him astray and so causing him to break a promise made to his mother/wife/patron saint, etc. Female Italian Seductors are very experienced, and may well leave you demanding more.

Italian Seductees also roll their eyes a lot. However, both male and female Seductees will accuse the Seductor of making them break a promise to their mothers/wives/husbands/patron saint, etc.

American Seductors are only ever female. Most American males have no opportunity for seduction, they're too busy being seduced. The rest regard it as unnecessary, unmanly and distinctly un-American. The truth is that any male given to wearing polyester suits would think that way.

American Seductees are, if male, often Mormon missionaries; if female, full of angst.

Overall, American seduction techniques are to do with being:
- misunderstood
- rich
- available.

South American Seductors are always fiercely passionate in a Latin sort of way (i.e. persistent, smooth and obvious). Both male and female consider it not so much a seduction, but a benediction, bestowed on the lucky Seductee.

South American Seductees are always female, since male pride can accept nothing less than the dominant role. Bluffers should know that female South American Seductees are always reluctant ... up to the final moment. Note, however, that none of the above applies to Brazil, where the last recorded seduction took place nearly a hundred years ago. The rest of the world has seductions, Brazil simply has sex.

Russian Seductors, if male, are serious and intense about the whole business. Female Seductors on the other hand are in it for the fun and games. While Russian male Seductors fall in love (or claim to do so) beforehand, females only ever do so afterwards, and always in a deeply spiritual manner.

Russian Seductees, if male, are convinced it was their idea in the first place. Very occasionally it was. Russian female Seductees will also fall in love, but in a far from spiritual manner.

Swedish Seductors and Seductees do not exist. Instead, relationships are formed with the intention of discussing the Third World Debt. The fact that nature then takes its course explains a good deal of the collective guilt felt in Sweden: for few couples get around to discussing the Third World Debt – unless, of course, they are being filmed for a documentary, in which case they talk of little else.

Bluffers should be aware that any attempt to play the Seductor or Seductee in a relationship with a Swede will be greeted with polite laughter and a mini lecture on safe sex.

Arab Seductors are inevitably male and given to long, soulful looks. Female Seductees in search of Fame and Fortune are advised to ignore the soulful look and hold out for the money.

Arab seduction techniques tend to be:
– passionate
– unexpected
– of short lived duration (sometimes of such short lived duration that the female Seductee is unaware that it's begun, let alone all over).

Arab Seductees of the female sort have been known to carry knives, or to have the services of bodyguards who carry knives. The male Arab Seductee is liable to be underage, but just as dangerous to your health. Bluffers are advised to scrupulously avoid both.

Irish Seductors, male and female, can be recognised by a roguish gleam in the eye. Both are given to Celtic flights of fancy and tend to operate in an honest-to-God open way, and at break-neck speed. (But not as quickly as Arabs.)

Irish Seductees, male and female, are given to long bouts of melancholy and reproachful glances. They are perfect victims for romantics, poets and martyrs.

Body Language

Bluffers must be aware of the importance of body language when dealing with a Foreign Seductor or Seductee. Many an otherwise promising occasion has been wrecked because, by innocently scratching one's nose, a mortal insult has been given to the Foreign Person sitting opposite, who may take it as a sign that they are:
- homosexual
- impotent
- desperate
- illegitimate

or all four at once.

The general rule is to follow the lead of the Foreign Person him or herself. However, this does not mean that you should:

a)   also explore your left ear
b)   pick your right nostril, or
c)   scratch reflectively at your crotch.

   At least, not in public.

Of course if the Foreign Person is doing one or all of those things in public, it really is time you Made Your Excuses and Left. Unless you are motivated by Fame and Fortune, in which case you should:

- applaud the natural spontaneity of your partner
- discreetly offer them a Kleenex
- run a quick check on their finances.

Bluffers should also be aware of those innocent gestures that, far from causing offence to the Foreign Person, will inflame him or her beyond all recognition. For example, winking lightheartedly at a male South American may result in endless flowers plus pictures (signed) of him playing polo, followed by a furtive tapping at your door at three in the morning. Winking at a female South American may result in a long, smouldering glance, followed by her father, uncle and brother beating your door down at three in the morning.

Similarly, any female slipping her arm companionably through that of an Arab (male) is likely to be force-marched to the nearest hotel. By the same token, a Swede may well misinterpret a passing interest in the Psychology of Depression as an invitation to who knows what? Of course, this is not body language as such, but it is the closest that most Swedes get.

SEDUCTIVE TYPES

Few professional Seductors or Seductees are recognisable as such. Amateurs always are. Bluffers should familiarise themselves with the most obvious types, if only to avoid them.

Professional:

The Roué (Seductor)

The silver-grey hair at his temple is as elegantly maintained as his clothes. And just as ancient. He plans on impressing the young with his experience, or the not-so-young with his energy. The Roué knows all the right questions to ask, but is not really listening; he's too busy fielding the admiring glances of other women. He drinks whisky, cultivates a mid-European accent and dines in hotel restaurants. Often ends his days as a convent handyman.

The Gigolo (Seductee)

Tries hard to look younger than the Seductor. Very occasionally he is. But his mental processes, such as they are, age rapidly. Gigolos set enormous store by their hair, taut muscles, flawless suntans and the ability to light a woman's cigarette at fifty paces. They are convinced they are devastatingly good-looking. Sometimes they are, but always in an obvious sort of way. As a professional Seductee, the Gigolo is something of a fraud, since everyone knows that he will succumb, it's just a matter of time. Either that, or start paying for his own clothes, holidays and champagne.

The Siren (Seductor)
Well dressed and invariably photographed through a soft focus lense to disguise the crows' feet. This woman is dynamite (her press agent says so) and can have her pick of any male, of any age, with an IQ lower than 100. She is rarely seen by day since it takes her many hours to make up, not with cosmetics but with her latest boyfriend after their well publicised fight in a fashionable restaurant the night before. She drinks mineral water, although will admit to liking cocktails, and vintage (always vintage) wine.

The Tease (Seductee)
This lady is actually a professional promiser. She has a range of facial expressions and seductive gestures or remarks that could inflame a monk. But the truth is that sex disgusts her. She can't bear to be reminded that she does actually sweat. The Tease is essentially genteel in the worst possible way. She drinks white wine, often mixed with Perrier, and spends long hours discussing with girlfriends how all men are 'such brutes'. This never stops her accepting dinner from a perfect (or near-perfect) stranger.

Amateur (Male):

The Lad About Town
Doesn't always wear a medallion around his neck, but would like to. He is given to crooning in your ear (usually out of tune) and may well be a good dancer. He doesn't really mind if he's the Seductor or Seductee, just so long as he's being noticed. Found in trendy discos (the barman knows him by name) and drinks elaborate cocktails. He'd rather drink beer.

The City Up-and-Comer
Ostensibly likes to be the Seductor, but since he is terrified of sex and women, will thankfully settle for being seduced . . . once only . . . he's in too much of a hurry for experience to try a return match. He is found in wine bars where he drinks champagne. He'd rather drink elaborate cocktails.

The Tortured Intellectual
Is often found on the heavily oversubscribed staff of a political weekly with falling circulation. He is, has been or is thinking about, becoming Left-wing. Will mutter about the latest unemployment statistics. Would like to be the Seductor, but considers it degrading to women. Would like to be seduced, but considers it a sign of weakness. Has a pretty poor sex life, really. Drinks beer, but would prefer champagne.

The Man of the World
Often tries to hide the fact that he is a good ten years older than he claims. Or if his real age is known, claims his extra years have given him so much more experience, savoir faire, etc. They haven't. Does suggestive things with bread-sticks at dinner, which is usually in a quite appalling restaurant where he's known (and loathed) by name. Always likes to be the Seductor, until he realises you've an IQ higher than 20, at which point he tends to withdraw. Drinks wine and insists on smelling the cork.

The Wild Colonial
Has raised naivety to an art form. Is often homesick after drinking too much – anything that's alcoholic and free. Never needs to be the Seductor: "It's all those sheilas after my body, y'know . . ."

Amateur (Female):

Benidorm Girl
Believes in her natural right to a year-round tan, from whatever source. She has a huge amount of street sense, but believes that seduction takes place after one or another of the parties has passed out from drink, which makes it okay. She is intensely romantic, especially about large diamond engagement rings. If she has one, she will contrive to wear it in such a way that it enters the room some seconds before she does. A natural born Seductee, she can be found wherever there's:
- a lot of noise
- repetitive music
- an endless supply of strange-coloured drinks.

The Vamp
Sees herself as a sensual tigress in search of her (male) prey. The truth is that she's really looking for someone who will bring her warm milk in bed. The Vamp may not necessarily advertise her persona by her clothes, but will give long, challenging glances. She can be found at every party making overtures to each man in turn, desperate to make sure she doesn't go home alone. She likes obscure drinks: enjoys going absinthe from work with her latest conquest.

Ms Successful
Has sacrificed everything for her career, but knows her ambitions will only truly be realised when the right man comes along. Until then she is ready to play the field as both Seductor and Seductee whenever a suitable candidate presents himself. She is perceptive, selective, and immaculately turned out. Her confidence enables her to drink anything from Campari to CocaCola, and pay for it.

The Good Sport
Knows that seduction is something that older men very properly do to girls like her. How else will she be able to show her own boyfriend what's required? She likes being appreciated for her:
- breeding
- maturity
- sensitivity
- and good looks

in that order. But she suffers from a secret fear that she is really only being entertained for her large Trust Fund.

She can be found loitering with intent to bray wherever a Royal is likely to show up. She bravely drinks whatever is put in front of her, but prefers it to be expensive.

The Innocent Abroad
Is easily impressed by almost anything. Her five year mission (before returning to her homeland and domesticity) is to boldly go where no woman has gone before. This means that the promise of an exclusive experience turns her into the most willing Seductee imaginable. She is extremely trusting but has a poor memory; drinks beer because gin makes her tipsy.

MEETING

Seductor meets Seductee. How that meeting takes place
will quickly prove whether you are:

1. a professional
2. an amateur
3. a public nuisance.

Of course, many Seductors and Seductees are introduced
by mutual friends. Others meet in the course of business.
One or two have met via the emotional Sits Vac columns.
Preferred professional meetings, however, take place:

- at first nights
- at artist's private views
- on an expensive street
- trekking in the Himalayas
- in a hot air balloon
- while waiting in the Green Room to appear on
  television
- walking along a deserted shore (Spring and
  Autumn only)
- on any international flight
- on the deck of an ocean liner
- at Charity events
- at the racetrack (cars or horses only)
- on the ski slopes
- at any kind of concert, even Rock
- at the supermarket (Safeways or Sainsbury is fine.
  Tesco doubtful. Asda, and you should be ashamed of
  yourself.)
- at the laundrette (so long as you've got interesting
  clothes)
- offering to share your taxi, or umbrella, when it's
  raining.

Opening Lines

As a professional bluffing Seductor you will be able to sum up the Seductee without even trying. You will know whether you're dealing with an amateur or a professional, and what their motives are likely to be. You will adjust your opening words accordingly. For example, confronted with:

A Professional (Ego) – admire something about them in a mildly self-deprecating way.

An Amateur (Ego) – enthuse irresistibly, about everything.

Professional (Force of Habit) – invite them for a drink with the style and assurance of one who knows that they'll say yes.

An Amateur (Force of Habit) – first pretend that you've both met before, and when that confusion has been cleared up, go for a drink.

Bluffers must remember that while Professionals know what is going on and are prepared to skip the opening niceties to a greater or lesser extent, Amateurs need a little preliminary skirmishing.

Never, ever, use hackneyed opening lines. If you can't think of anything outstanding to say, it doesn't matter. Nobody ever came unstuck with 'How do you do' as a starter. Leave witty remarks to those Amateur Seductors who buy books on the subject and practise while doing their teeth. Remember the rule of the art is that seductions should never look as if they started out that way; the Seductee has to be allowed some measure of self-respect.

When declaring your hand it is important to bear in mind the essential ingredient of any seduction, namely that while the Seductor is interested, the Seductee is not, for whatever reason. As a result the Seductor's first task is to:

1. Establish contact in a non-threatening sort of way. ("Hi, babe, fancy a quickie?" would not be considered suitable.)
2. Establish that you are interested in the Seductee as a person, and that a distinct possibility exists that you might even admire the Seductee's mind.
3. Find a legitimate reason for meeting again, which has nothing to do with sex.

Bluffers must know that while it is not a good idea to sexually confront a Seductee in the initial stages, it is even worse to do so if the Seductee's lover is also present. Unless of course, the Seductee is obviously just a little bit bored with his or her company. Top marks are rightly given to the Seductor who manages to attract the attention of the Seductee in, say, a crowded restaurant, and proposition them without the hapless lover knowing what's going on. One legendary Seductor who managed to do this, subsequently achieving the object of his desire, took the Seductee back to the same restaurant for a celebratory meal. It happened that the (by now) ex-lover was also there, dining with business friends. The ex-lover fumed loudly. The Seductor smiled gently, ordered a bowl of grapes, poured vinegar over them and sent it to the ex-lover's table: sour grapes.

Especially Seductive Places

Classic seductions must involve, at some time, the ritual of Eating Out. Bluffers should know that a modern school of Seductors holds that the more outlandish the restaurant, the greater the chance of success. Their idea is that the Seductee will be so shell-shocked at being whisked away to eat curried goat in Brixton that all resistance will crumble; especially if dressed up for the occasion.

Similarly, the young school of Seductors believes that Eating Out should involve champagne and strawberries on a warm day by the river. You can point out that:

a) eating curried goat surrounded by Rastafarians suspicious of people in evening dress is not conducive to anything, other than a swift retreat.

b) while champagne and strawberries are available the year round, in Britain warm days are not. Besides, rivers these days are likely to be full of anglers wrestling with angry carp; and the banks besieged by determined-looking ramblers.

Every bluffing Seductor should know a few of the ideal places for a seduction to take place. You might never make use of any of them, but to drop them into the conversation at a suitable opportunity can't fail to give the impression that you do.

1. Dinner in New York, having flown there by Concorde, and a hotel in Connecticut after dinner, having travelled there by private helicopter.

2. A cottage where the moors run down to the sea which is fully equipped with hot running water, the latest in sound systems and oil lamps. Very romantic, oil lamps.

3. A boat. Not a floating gin palace, but a rather elderly, classic yacht (wood throughout) that never actually leaves harbour.

4. The back of a stretch limousine driving down Park Lane ... and along Knightsbridge ... and down to the Kings Road ... and back up Sloane Street ... and twice round the Park, preferably during rush hour.

5. A box at Convent Garden, when Placido Domingo is singing *Don Giovanni*.

6. A stalled lift.

But never, ever, on the beach. This will show your ignorance, for any true professional knows that sand is an abrasive. And that it gets simply everywhere.

Dealing With Difficult Situations

One of the main differences between a Professional and an Amateur is that the Professional always knows how to put the situation right when it starts to go wrong, whereas the Amateur has to abandon the attempted seduction and start all over again. There are some classic situations that every Seductor may well meet, and here are some notable examples.

Situation
The Seductee (female, amateur) tearfully states in the middle of dinner that she can't stop thinking about the boyfriend who recently jilted her.

The Amateur Seductor would:
a) ask all about her recent affair
b) offer her brotherly solace and understanding
c) take her home.

The Professional Seductor would:
a) invent an ex-lover who betrayed him in a far worse manner
b) order an extra bottle of something expensive and toast 'absent friends'
c) suggest they spend the weekend together, in Paris, in order to forget.

Situation

The Seductor and Seductee are on their first date together. In a crowded place, they are accosted by a Noisy and Glamorous Person who talks enthusiastically of a date with the Seductor/Seductee the following evening.

The Amateur Seductor(ee) will:
– blush
– introduce everyone
– abruptly excuse him/herself to take refuge in the cloakroom
– end up alone, or with two companions, that night.

The Professional Seductor(ee) will:
– say "Didn't you get my message – I can't make tomorrow, I'm afraid."
– spill his or her drink all over the Noisy and Glamorous Person which hastens their departure
– make a quick decision as to who is likely to be the most fun or most rewarding, which might mean leaving the original date to make his/her own way home.

Situation

The Seductee arrives unexpectedly at the Seductor's home – complete with toothbrush and overnight bag. Normally the Seductor would be delighted (although surprised, since they only met the previous evening) except that:
- the house is in chaos, and the Seductee obviously fastidious
- the house is still being occupied by an ex-husband/wife/lover who is taking time about moving out, and who is unpleasant and jealous
- the Seductor doesn't really live at that address but is simply house-sitting for some rich friends who are expected back at any time.

The Amateur Seductor would:
- say "Look, this is far too soon . . . I'll call you later."
- hope the Seductee will take one look and go away
- tell the truth.

The Professional Seductor would:
- explain that the house has been lived in by a family of political refugees (just departed for a new life in America) and get the Seductee to tidy up
- lock the ex-wife/husband/lover in the basement, and blame the strange bangings and shrill cries for help on a neighbour's radio or television
- install the Seductee, and when the rightful house owners return, explain that the house has been commandeered by the Anti-Terrorist Squad who are watching a particularly dangerous group of terrorists opposite.

Situation

The Seductor and Seductee (female) are enjoying dinner

together when the Seductee spots a Friend of her husband in the same restaurant.

The Amateur Seductor would:
- worry the entire evening
- slide slowly under the table in an attempt to hide
- call for the bill and leave.

The Professional Seductor would:
- make a pass at the Friend
- ring up another person and invite him or her to join them
- send a bottle of champagne to the Friend in the Seductee's name, complete with a saucy suggestion.

Situation
The Seductor discovers that he has left his wallet at home:

The Amateur:
- apologises profusely to everyone
- allows the Seductee to pay
- does the washing-up in the restaurant kitchen.

The Professional:
- convinces the restaurant that he is a food critic, and reluctantly allows the restaurant to pick up the tab
- telephones an anonymous bomb threat (NB: Italian restaurants will, however, usually ask patrons to pay their bills before allowing them to escape.)
- allows the Seductee to believe that the only reason the wallet was left at home was so that the Seductee would have to go there in order to get her money back.

SHE SEDUCES HIM

He is trying to get over a broken love affair. His ex-girl friend has gone off with a man who is:
- richer
- older
- better looking
- fond of climbing Mount Everest as a hobby
- the author of a best-selling book of poetry
- an ex-champion athlete, now TV celebrity
- reputedly wonderful in bed;

any one of which is designed to reduce the average (spurned) male ego to a gooey smear on the pavement of life (spurned men often talk like that, too).

You, the Seductor, have known and, if not loved, at least been enamoured of him, for some time. It's not that you want to bring solace into his life, so much as bring a certain something into your own. And why not? If all goes according to plan, he won't worry about whether your intentions are honourable or not.

However, his confidence is at an all-time low. He is too demoralised even to play the 'Poor Me' role that most men find second nature. And by the time he gets out of that, the chances are that another woman may well have him in her sights. Nonetheless, he may well be expecting some sort of approach from a woman, in accordance with Masculine Lore and Legend. If so, he will secretly be dreading it happening because he really doesn't feel up to it.

All of which means that the seduction must be:
1. well planned
2. non-confrontational
3. well executed.

Above all, it must not even resemble a seduction.

The Setting

The setting must always be your own home. If you 'share' it, bribe whoever to leave for the night (and most of the next day. You may get luckier than you expect). If you have a boyfriend, wait until he's out of the country. If you're married, well, shame on you. But wait until your husband is at least out of town for the weekend. Remember that a recently cuckolded male can show a certain reluctance to do the same to another of his sex. If you suspect this might be the case, let him know some time beforehand that you're experiencing marital difficulties.

The Occasion

This should appear to be totally innocent, not a formal invitation to dinner, for if he suspects what is intended his subsequent nervousness may result in a poor performance in direct ratio to the amount of trouble you've taken. So the invitation is either:

casual – for example if you both play squash together (but don't tire the poor dear out) and he drops you off at home.

business – assuming you work together or in a related field.

accidental – as when you run into him in a local pub, purely by 'chance'.

comic – if he lives next door for example, and you discover a spider in the bath, or need a plug fixing.
(NB: the only trouble with the 'spider in the bath' routine is that:
a.   you have to go out and buy one
b.   he might think you're a complete dingbat
c.   he might just kill it and then walk out.)

The Preparations

Try to ensure that when the Seductee does arrive, he'll find your home appreciably different from the one he shared with his Lost Love. If she was tidy, scatter a few clothes around. If she was untidy, try to produce something that would look good enough for a spread in *House and Garden*. If your own abode is simply beyond salvage, you can always blow the fuses and operate in pitch blackness alleviated only by a few romantic and strategically-placed candles. The point is to produce an environment that:

a) will not remind him of 'home'
b) will mark you as an 'interesting' person
c) does not scream seduction at every turn.

Food and drink are easy:

Drink: Imported beers – for a little touch of luxury that will impress – and a good white wine cooling in the fridge. (Remember men just know that women can't choose a decent red wine.)

Food: Good and plain, nothing that:

a. will take too long to serve
b. looks too carefully chosen
c. will mean exile to the living room while you cook.

For if he's exiled, he will begin to brood. Then, when you enter triumphantly bearing a dish of Les Ravioles de Truffes à la Crème de Mousserons (truffle ravioli in a wild mushroom sauce) it will be to find him sunk deep into melancholy and your favourite armchair. And it will prove impossible to move him from either.

The Arrival

This is probably the most crucial stage of the entire night. For, in the space of a few minutes, you have to:

1. make him feel completely at ease
2. establish that you're running the show, but not in a manner that's going to intimidate him
3. get him thinking, even unconsciously, about sex.

So, as soon as he crosses your threshold, offer him a drink, one that he has to get himself from the fridge. Because you're:

a) just finishing changing, or
b) in the middle of a phone call.

Tell him to help himself and, while he's about it, get one for you.

There is something surprisingly intimate about allowing a comparative stranger access to your fridge. A person's fridge can tell someone else more about their character, financial state and habits, than anything else. And here you are, offering this man access to your innermost domestic secrets. And in the kitchen, too, which makes the whole scene safe, or rather, friendly. Let a man into your kitchen and your fridge and he'll trust you forever – plus in this instance, he'll also notice the food. Men who are pining might not think they feel like eating, but food prepared by someone else has an amazing effect on the libido.

Meanwhile, you have changed into your old trousers, most comfortable skirt, or even a genuine kaftan, but never jeans. You might look great in denim, but when push comes to shove and clothes need to be shed, few people can surreptitiously, or seductively, get out of a pair of jeans.

The Seduction

You are now ready to proceed slowly and inexorably to the final stage. Begin by talking to him about almost anything, except his past love, otherwise he may:

- become tearful
- mentally compare you with her
- get so fraught he'll spill beer on your carpet.

Talk about yourself. Talk about mutual friends. Talk about films, music or television. But switch the subject rapidly as soon as you see him become pensive, for it means a memory has been triggered by the mention of something that He Shared With Her.

If you have business to discuss, do so. If there's a plug for him to fix, get him to move a bookshelf or two as well. Make him feel useful, to the world in general, and you in particular.

At some stage, move towards the kitchen saying "Hold on, I'll get us something to eat". Notice that a good bluffing Seductor does not ask *if* he wants to eat: you take it for granted. And after you've been in the kitchen for a few minutes, call out for him to "Come and talk to me while I'm doing this". When he comes, you get him another drink and let him watch you work. Remember that you must:

a) find a reason for pressing close to him, say in reaching for a kitchen utensil or the oregano
b) ask him to do at least one simple task (open the wine, for instance, or refill the pepper grinder).

Most men find the sight of an attractive woman fixing a meal quite sexy. It makes them feel pampered, and since it's in the kitchen Seductees won't feel sexually threatened.

Get him to lay the table ('set' the table if he is American). Find time to give your neck and wrists a going-over with the scent bottle; and then bring out the food, and keep his glass filled. Don't let him talk about himself – he'll bring the subject round to Her Who Done Him Wrong. The meal over, produce a bottle of good brandy, and choose a record, nothing too schmaltzy (never

Leonard Cohen or Dory Previn who will have him in tears inside in ten seconds).

There you are, both sitting comfortably. Now you begin: "I'm so glad you came round. I haven't felt this relaxed in ages . . . But I can see there's something troubling you." This is the coup de grâce. All evening the poor man has been longing to talk about his broken heart. All evening you've headed him off. Now he's relaxed and feeling better than he has done in ages (well, at least the past week) and suddenly you, his comforter, bring him back to earth.

He will appear to be reluctant to talk. "Come on," you say, "come and sit next to me and tell me all about it." And he will. Your only trouble will be in getting him to stop. But let him talk. It gives you the excuse to hold his hand. If he cries a little, brush away the tears with your fingers. And watch him carefully because:

- at some stage he's going to be aware that this sympathetic woman who smells divine is sitting very, very close
- he doesn't want to go home alone
- he doesn't know if he dares to make what he thinks are the first advances.

When this point is reached, lean forward, cup his face with your hands and kiss him gently. Murmur something like "I always swore I'd never get involved like this . . . but you are so terribly attractive."

He will now:
a)   return your kiss with interest
b)   go limp
c)   leap to his feet with a shrill cry and rush to the door.
The first two are fine. The last means that you're left with the washing-up.

Assuming he's still there, get to your feet (slowly), take him by the hand and lead him to your bedroom. If he tries to say anything, hush him with a finger to his lips.

The Denouement

The bedroom is softly lit, with the bedcover turned down. Too many women have faltered at this last hurdle by going through the elaborate process of:

- taking the cover off and carefully folding it
- worrying about which side he prefers
- fussing about the candles
- setting the alarm clock, and
- plumping up the pillows.

Remember this is a seduction, not a military operation (even if you did plan it that way). Similarly, it would be a trifle insensitive to press a packet of condoms in his hand, smile archly and say "Well, you know what those are for." Of course he does, they're for putting over the heads of women who make silly remarks.

Sit him on the bed and carefully, unhurriedly, undress him. Never let his eyes leave yours. For every bit of clothing you remove, take a bit off too . . . and the rest is up to you.

There are, however, two remaining rules:

1. Never let him know it was all your idea in the first place. He'll suspect it, will secretly be delighted, but tell him, and he'll leave you.

2. He must stay the full night. If he leaves in the small hours of the morning to return to his own empty abode, he'll brood a bit, trying to remember what She was like, and later, with his new-found confidence, go out and find someone new. And it won't be you.

HE SEDUCES HER

He is motivated by Lust. She is the most stunning woman he has ever laid eyes on.

She is motivated by Ego tinged with Curiosity. She knows she is stunning. She is the most stunning woman she knows.

The Seductor is professional; the Seductee is amateur. The stage is set for a perfect bluffing seduction.

The Setting

This must always be:

First – an intimate, but fashionable, restaurant, though not so fashionable that she spends her time looking at other diners.

Second – your flat or home. Never, in this instance, a hotel unless you:

a) have a permanent suite reserved at the Savoy
b) can afford to fly somewhere interesting, like Paris, or New York, in your own private jet
c) have a girlfriend/wife/teenagers waiting up for you (in which case, claim storm damage).

NB: If a hotel is to be used, you must ensure that everything has been arranged for in your name before the evening commences. Many a seduction has been ruined by the embarrassment caused when Seductor and Seductee check in under separate names and the desk clerk leers knowingly.

The Occasion

The occasion should simply be that you enjoy her company. No subterfuge is necessary. Make your intentions known from the start, then if she accepts, it means she's half way interested, or desperate for a good meal.

However, no good bluffer would ever admit in advance that he expected the Seductee to fall instantly for his charms. A certain amount of modest reticence is called for. In fact points can be given for:

1. Being just a little impassive – i.e. you're not very bothered either way . . . but it would be nice
2. Having an alternative Seductee in mind.

The Preparations

These are straightforward, and formal. The point is to impress upon the Seductee that you:

a) care about her
b) know how to enjoy yourself
c) have a good deal of style
d) are used to entertaining a 'special' woman.

Remember that a woman can only determine how you're likely to behave in more intimate circumstances by how you behave with her in public. You will therefore have to show thoughtfulness from the start.

So, do not arrange to meet at the restaurant. Infer that you're bound to be late (i.e. you would not want her waiting alone, the target of unwanted attentions, or waiter's sneers). Instead, hire a chauffeur-driven limousine. It's gaudy but impressive, and you won't have to worry about drinking and driving. Better still, send the limousine for her (she can't fail to enjoy the solitary luxury and will feel both pampered and important), and have it pick you up:

– outside the Houses of Parliament
– in front of the Bank of England
– at the door of the Foreign Office.

Claim, and apologise for, pressure of work. If asked what work, invoke the Official Secrets Act.

The Arrival

The restaurant will have been paid in advance, to ensure that you are:
a) greeted by name
b) given a good table
c) allowed to sign the bill at the end.
Bluffers are aware that anyone can have a credit card; almost anyone can have a gold credit card; but only special people get to sign the bill.

You will also have organised flowers for her, at the table. Nothing too extravagant (e.g. gladioli), but different from any other flowers at adjacent tables. A solitary orchid would do, although you are advised to avoid the obvious blooms. Roses are always safe, but a little posy of wild flowers (violets, primroses) would work wonders. A potted hyacinth, however nice as a trophy, is likely to leak muddy water when moved.

When choosing from the menu, you should be attentive to her wishes. Assume openly that she knows all about food, wine and whether, say, fugu fish are in season. Nevertheless, do not let the burden of choosing a meal fall upon the Seductee. Help in her selection, and if she's not sure about something ask the waiter to explain the dish "Would you mind telling us . . ." and look carefully at her, not the menu, while it's described. In this way it is apparent to all that you know what's what, you're merely being discreet.

If she decides rapidly or without assistance, establish your authority; for instance, by indicating the Salade de Homard en Bolero (lobster salad with tomato, avocado and apple) and asking the waiter "What sort of apples are you using for the lobster salad?" Aside from anything else, this kind of thing will probably put the waiter at a disadvantage, resulting in a trail of others, possibly even the Head Waiter, which is guaranteed to impress the Seductee.

Bluffers will, of course, have obtained a copy of the menu some days beforehand and learnt it by heart. They will also know:

- the name of the Chef
- the name of the Head Waiter
- what the truly best dishes are, as opposed to those that the restaurant is trying to push because someone ordered too many morels.

Conversation during the meal should be entirely about her. If you've done your job well so far, there will be no need to add anything to the picture she has formed about you. Instead, let her impress you a little. Be interested in her mind, and never her décolletage, although you can allow her to catch you looking at her in a speculative sort of way. One that denotes a certain sexual interest on your part. When and if this happens, smile charmingly and change the subject.

You will have ordered a white, or a light red wine to go with the meal (never a heavy claret or burgundy since this can easily encourage drowsiness and thoughts of sleeping, *only* sleeping, which will never do.) If you can, order champagne. But never Dom Perignon, since this is extremely expensive, overrated, and the one chosen in American soap operas. Instead, go for one like the vintage Perrier Jouet Bell Epoque, which comes in an unusual art nouveau bottle. This gives you the opportunity to display:

1. your good taste in wine
2. your refusal to follow the herd.

The Move

The move is made over coffee and liqueurs. You will flatter her (but not outrageously) and turn the conversation to more intimate matters, e.g.

- her eyes
- her smile
- her sensuality.

At some stage, include the beauty of her hands since this will allow you to stroke the underside of her wrist, very gently, with the tips of your fingers. But never for too long. The crunch point, in fact, will come when you close your own hand over hers. If she leaves her hand there, or returns the pressure:

a) contain yourself
b) confess how seductive you find her
c) order more champagne.

If she whisks her hand away as if it was stung:

a) employ one of the get-out phrases used by bluffers to keep their integrity intact
b) excuse yourself for a few minutes to call up a long-standing girlfriend to find out if it's not too late to see what she's doing for the rest of the evening.

Assuming your interest is returned, you are now about to reach the most challenging part of the evening.

The Finale

This has to be judged finely, because it involves:

a) the masterful assumption that you are going to spend the rest of the night together
b) the sensitive awareness that the Seductee wants to make up her own mind

c) the necessity to declare your hand whatever the outcome.

Bear in mind that many a Seductor has failed simply because he feared rejection and decided at the last to keep the Big Question for another day. Remember that:

- faint heart ne'er won fair lady
- each trial seduction adds to your store of experience
- it's not too late to call up what's-her-name.

Ideally, the proposition should come not so much in words as in looks. Intense eye-to-eye contact . . . warm smiles . . . appraising glances. If you can't tell from the way she's looking at you whether she's amenable or not, you're no real bluffer. And certainly not a professional Seductor.

However you can test for the right response by breaking off in the middle of your conversation and suddenly looking at her with burning intensity. If she continues with friendly but polite conversation, realise that she's a true Professional or shy or very stupid. If she returns your gaze with equal intensity and accompanies it with a low, sweet smile that sends your pulses racing – then you're away.

Call for the bill (which you sign), take her by the hand and lead her from the restaurant. The car awaits. Either that, or the restaurant is a short walking distance from home . . . where you have a bottle of Benedictine, vintage brandy, or hot chocolate (imported, Dutch, and a well-known aphrodisiac) which may act as:

- a relaxant, or
- a celebration,

and hopefully, both.

USEFUL WORDS AND PHRASES

There is no question but that any professional Seductor or Seductee must have a complete mastery of seductive language – those words and phrases that will allow you to:

1. Make your pitch (Getting In).
2. Retire gracefully (Getting Out).

You will notice that the sheer joy of many of these words and expressions is that they are almost interchangeable; and the basic vocabulary is not all that extensive.

However, you must also know that the effectiveness of seductive language also depends on its delivery, and that there are four basic delivery modes:

• The Blurt

• The Smoulder

• The Snatch

• The Muse.

The Blurt is a statement that comes from nowhere. It is totally unexpected, might be delivered in the middle of a conversation about, say, the best mulch for begonias, and signifies that whoever is making it (Seductor or Seductee) has been overcome by passion and depth of feelings.

The Smoulder relies on strong eye contact, is delivered slowly, and is wrecked by even the merest hint of amusement from either party. It signifies that the

Seductor/Seductee is ready to make his her final moves and should never be used unless you are sure of receiving a favourable response.

The Snatch is, as its name implies, quite physical. It involves grabbing hold (but gently) of one part or another of your partner's anatomy (but nowhere too intimate, please), and speaking quickly and urgently to her or him. It does not take the speaker by surprise, as does The Blurt, since he or she will have been steeling themselves to speak thus for some time – an obvious preparation – so that whoever is on the receiving end can feign surprise without being genuinely unprepared.

The Muse is the statement that tests the water. It is delivered almost in the form of a question that tails gently off, and is said as if the speaker is almost talking to him or her self. Eye contact is reduced to a quick, surreptitious flash during The Muse to see how the other is taking it. And, if they are taking it in the way it is intended, a full and frank stare at its end.

Getting In

You make me feel so:

alive	(Snatch)
loving	(Smoulder)
needed	(Blurt)
special	(Muse)

Getting Out

You make me feel so:

old/experienced	(Blurt)
responsible	(Muse)
inadequate	(Muse)
unworthy	(Snatch)

NB: Note that the Smoulder is never used in Getting Out, since it will invariably be misinterpreted as a come-on. It should also be understood that a minimum amount of eye-contact is used in Getting Out, and that whoever is trying to do so should look vaguely embarrassed, since this will make the other person feel guilty.

Getting In

You are simply/utterly:

amazing	(short Smoulder)
fantastic	(Blurt)
wonderful	(Smoulder)
masculine/feminine	(Muse)
incredible	(Snatch)

Getting Out

You are totally/always so:

understanding	(Muse)
charming	(Blurt)
your own person	(Snatch)
forgiving	(bored Muse)

Getting In

Could you ever:

love me?	(Blurt/Snatch)
feel the same way about me?	(Muse)
put up with me?	(Muse)
enjoy making love so intensely you forget your own name?	(long Smoulder)

Getting Out

Could you ever:

agree to my mother living with us?	(Blurt)
accept that I'm naturally unfaithful?	(Muse)
believe that Herpes isn't always contagious?	(Snatch)

Getting In

You remind me of:

that person in my dreams	(Muse)
an unfolding flower	(Smoulder)
someone who's been terribly hurt	(Blurt)
an ideal I never thought I'd find	(Snatch)

Getting Out

You remind me of:

my mother/father	(Muse)
someone who hurt me	(Blurt)
a person I met in prison	(Snatch)
my ex-lover/husband/wife	(Muse)

Getting In

I can tell by looking at you that:

you love being stroked	(Smoulder)
you've been so hurt	(Snatch)
you've never been totally loved	(Muse)
you want me as much as I want you	(Blurt)

Getting Out

I can tell by looking at you that:

you know this is wrong/has to end/is a mistake:	(Muse)
you want/don't want children	(Blurt)
you're ready to commit yourself totally to me	(Snatch)
you're still thinking of him/her – and I can't handle that	(Blurt)

Getting In

You're the only one who:

understands me	(Blurt)
could ever capture my heart	(Smoulder)
I've ever wanted so much that it hurts	(Snatch)
has ever made me want to change	(Muse)

Getting In

You're the only one who:

understands me too well	(Muse)
makes me feel so inadequate	(Blurt)
makes me wish I was somewhere else	(Snatch)
I know will enjoy train spotting	(Blurt)

Additionally, bluffers should also be aware of certain valuable Get Out statements that have become independent clasics over the years. For example:

"My husband/wife knows all about us – and aproves."

"My boyfriend has just been chosen for the International Karate Team, so we'll have lots more time together."

"My analyst wants to meet you."

"Can you cash me a cheque?"

"I don't want to spoil our friendship."

"You're just too intense for me."

"Do you believe that a person can love two separate people at the same time?"

"You're very special to me in ways that you'll never understand."

"I know that I'll only destroy you – and I think too much of you for that."

"My husband/wife is threatening to leave and take the kids." This is a complete killer, especially if it is the first time the other person has heard that:

   a. you are married
   b. you have kids
   c. they might be involved in a messy divorce.

THE AUTHOR

Yves Chébran drew on the experience of several wives (some of them his own), and a few interesting encounters in order to write this book. He wishes it to be known, however, that nowadays he is effectively retired. It might not be so much fun, but it is far less expensive. In time he hopes to reinstate his credit rating.

He would like to dedicate this book to all those women who knew exactly what was going on – but had the decency and tact to pretend they didn't.

THE BLUFFER'S GUIDES®

Available at £1.99 and *£2.50 each:

Accountancy*

Advertising*

Antiques

Archaeology*

Astrology & Fortune Telling

Ballet

Bluffing*

British Class

Champagne*

Chess*

Classics*

Computers*

Consultancy*

Cricket*

Doctoring*

Economics*

European Union*

Finance*

Flight Deck*

Golf*

Jazz*

Journalism

Law*

Literature

Management*

Marketing*

Maths

Modern Art*

Music*

Occult

Opera*

Paris*

Philosophy*

Photography

Poetry

P.R.*

Public Speaking*

Publishing

Races*

Rock Music Business*

Rugby*

Science*

Secretaries*

Seduction*

Sex*

Skiing*

Small Business*

Teaching*

Theatre

University*

Whisky*

Wine*

All these books are available at your local bookshop or newsagent, or by post or telephone from: B.B.C.S., P.O.Box 941, Hull HU1 3VQ. (24 hour Telephone Credit Card Line: 01482 224626)

Please add the following for postage charges: UK (& BFPO) Orders: £1.00 for the first book & 50p for each additional book up to a maximum of £2.50; Overseas (& Eire) Orders: £2.00 for the first book, £1.00 for the second & 50p for each additional book.